Daily Pacifiers for Busy Moms

If you would like information on Colleen's seminars or tapes, please contact her at:

Colleen Mountain
P.O. Box 80906
R.S.M., CA 92688-0906

Daily Pacifiers for Busy Moms

Lighthearted Encouragement for Mothers of Young Children

Colleen Mountain

HORIZON BOOKS
CAMP HILL, PENNSYLVANIA

Horizon Books
3825 Hartzdale Drive
Camp Hill, PA 17011
www.cpi-horizon.com

ISBN: 0-88965-144-2

98 99 00 01 02   5 4 3 2 1

Cover art by Ron Wheeler

Dedicated to

my precious little angel baby

Kirsty Angel Mountain

"For I know the plans I have for you," declares the LORD, "plans to prosper you and not to harm you, plans to give you hope and a future." (Jeremiah 29:11)

Contents

Foreword

Growing up, I couldn't wait to become a mother. That lofty title seemed like the most wonderful accomplishment that I could attain. When I first had difficulty becoming pregnant, I was frantic that I might not reach that wonderful goal.

When I was able to become pregnant, I was thrilled. God had given me a wonderful gift. When Darcy was born, my joy could not have been greater. I was finally a mother, and I just knew that years of fulfillment and love had begun . . . until Darcy turned nineteen months.

Suddenly, the joys of motherhood were elusive and undefinable. Darcy was no longer my smiling Gerber baby: she wanted to rule the roost. Temper tantrums were the order of the day. (Darcy had more than I did!) And I was shocked when she didn't want to cooperate with my plans for toilet training. Didn't she know that I wanted only the best for her? I was stressed out! I wanted to resign from motherhood!

If only I had available to me the book you hold, *Daily Pacifiers for Busy Moms*. I would have been able to handle the stresses of motherhood much better.

How is your stress level as a mom right now? Are you eyeing your child's pacifier with jealousy, wondering, *How can I get the same peaceful look on my face that's on that child right now?*

The answer is in your hands! You are in for a treat! With wisdom, humor and joy, *Daily Pacifiers for Busy Moms* will lighten your load and bring back your smile.

Colleen Mountain has a unique way of taking the stress out of mothering by turning it into thanksgiving to God. Whether she's addressing grocery shopping, priorities or "taming the tube," you'll come away refreshed in your mothering style.

I love Colleen's ability to be real in what she shares. As a mother, I appreciate writers and speakers who talk about mothering's "real" heart. When my children were young, I thought I had to be perfect. Such unrealistic expectations put even more stress on me and created more of a sense of failure.

But *Daily Pacifiers for Busy Moms* will not load you up with more unrealistic expectations. Instead, you'll experience the refreshing sharing of a real-life mom talking about real-life situations with real-life reassurance. Whether you read a little or a lot, you'll know that you can succeed as a mom.

Colleen has even been sensitive to your time pressures. Each mom-sized vignette will take only a few minutes to read and digest. And then she helps you to see "God's pacifier" in her experience so that you'll leave each story with a bit of encouragement.

Are you ready to put on that same contented look that your child has while sucking on a pacifier? Then read on!

Kathy Collard Miller
Author, speaker, mother

Acknowledgments

My husband, Rick—thanks for taking all those yellow legal pads and putting the stories into the computer. Thanks for believing in my dreams and encouraging me. I love you! xoxo

My friend, Christie Runion—thanks for listening, reading and all the girl talk. I appreciate the time you invested into this book and our friendship.

My dad—thanks for asking me umpteen times if I've sent those stories to a publisher.

My children, Kirsty and Luke—thanks for inspiring me to be the "best mom in the whole world." Hey, you guys need to tell me that even when I don't take you to McDonald's®. xoxo

My editor at Horizon Books, Janet—thanks for making me look good on paper. Thanks for your fun, honest approach on this book.

My once-upon-a-time Bible study group, Kim, Cindy, Jane and Marlene—you gals have influenced me more than you'll ever know! Thanks for being my friends.

My church family—thanks for allowing me the privilege of serving alongside you. May every boy and girl who comes onto our campus see Him through our love and service.

Introduction

This experience called motherhood is by far the greatest challenge yet. What do I mean by challenge? Think about it: Motherhood is the *one* experience that lasts a lifetime, has no formal training and no preview of coming attractions (like the movie theater has—where you can decide not to see a particular movie if it doesn't interest you!). Nope. When you see that little white strip turn blue, you have bought your ticket into motherhood. No refunds, no exchanges, no turning back, no way out. From that moment on, you are "Mom."

I can still remember the night I told Rick he was going to be a father. I got out the good china (who has bad china?). We had a romantic dinner, just the two of us. (Those were the days.) As he took his last bite of chicken, I told him, "Rick, you're going to be a dad!" He was speechless. He kept asking me if I was sure. Rick's response went something like, "How did—when did—where—I'm going to have a baby!!" My response was, "Actually, I will carry the baby for nine months and deliver the baby, but *you* can get up with me in the middle of the night and change diapers, feed the baby and give her a pacifier." My experience with pacifiers began early in motherhood. Here is one of my earliest memories.

Running across the store parking lot. Groceries in the cart. The baby in one arm. The diaper bag over one shoulder and purse over the other. And what does Kirsty do? Drops her pacifier! On top of all that, it's starting to sprinkle. A very nice lady stops and picks up the pacifier and, with no free hands, I ask her to put it in my mouth. I make up the excuse that I'm just going to clean the dirt off for Kirsty.

Instead, without thinking, I kept that hot pink thing in my mouth all the way home. Guess what I started looking for when I got home? Yep, the pacifier—which was in my mouth all along. And it's still only morning. What would my afternoon bring? Please God, let it bring a long nap.

Babies have their pacifiers for security. They have their blankies, bottles, special toy and, better yet, they have their mommies. What about Mom?

Where is her pacifier? Sometimes we need a *mom*-sized pacifier just to get through the hectic days and sleepless nights.

Here are some examples of mom-sized pacifiers.

- You get the last piece of dessert.

- You find a $20 bill in your other purse.

- You hit all the green lights.

- You step on the scale three pounds lighter.

- You come home to a clean house.

- You get an unexpected card of appreciation in the mail.

- You get a great parking space.

- You like the way you look in your new bathing suit.

- You wake up feeling rested.

- It's a good hair day.

- Your husband offers to go shopping with you.

- It's a beautiful weekend.

- Your girlfriend calls you from out of state.

- Your dressing room mirror is the kind that makes you look thinner.

- You don't have to buy formula anymore.

- Your friend brings a box of baby clothes over.
- You come home and there are no messages on the answering machine.
- You don't owe too much in taxes.
- You can curl up with a good book.
- Your husband takes you out to dinner.
- No one is on the equipment that you want at the gym.
- Grandma and Grandpa baby-sit.
- Your favorite craft store is having a fifty-percent-off sale.
- You're sitting in a Jacuzzi with no kids.
- Your baby is taking a long nap.
- Your baby can finally sit up in the grocery cart.
- You hear the word "Mom" for the first time.
- Your hair is finally long enough to put in a ponytail again.
- Your husband changes the diaper.
- Your friends at church bring meals the first week after the baby arrives.
- You leave your discount warehouse club and spent less than $100.

- Your little one toddles around with a smiling face.

- Your plants are still alive after the summer.

- The neighbor's dog has laryngitis.

- You have fresh flowers for your office or kitchen.

- You finally take all the extra stuff stacked in your garage to Good Will.

- There's hot water left after your husband takes his shower.

- You're all packed, getting into the car to take off for the weekend.

- You climb into bed after a long day.

- You're at the movies and the baby that's fussing is not yours.

May I add, before we continue, that you have the single most important job that ever existed on earth. As a mother, you are a motivator, coach, nurse, teacher, counselor, janitor, fashion consultant, chef and wife—which comes with its own set of duties to fulfill. I like to think of myself as CEO of Mountain Incorporated along with Rick, my husband. I set the pace for our family and set a vision for each new year. Often it is up to me to keep the Mountains going in the right direction. I can honestly say there is no greater joy than loving my family and fulfilling my role as wife and mother.

Enjoy as you read a bit of my journey into motherhood.

Blessings,
Colleen Mountain

day 1

A House with a View

I know what it is to be in need, and I know what it is to have plenty. I have learned the secret of being content in any and every situation, whether well fed or hungry, whether living in plenty or in want. (Philippians 4:12)

Rick and I are in the process of preparing to buy our first home. This is no easy feat when you live in Southern California. (Homes here are very expensive!) We've thought about moving to Colorado, but when you've been raised in a particular area, you tend to stay. Besides, both our parents live near us now. They are truly our favorite pacifier.

Our one-bedroom apartment is closing in on us. No, not from an earthquake. The crib is in the family room filled with Kirsty's toys, which her grandparents lavish on her, not knowing we don't have the room for them.

Rick and I have the perfect house all picked out. It's in a nice neighborhood, has good schools and a small yard (which is OK with us . . . less yard work). Then we looked at the house right across the street and guess what it had? It had a beautiful view of the Saddleback Mountains. I stopped for a moment and visualized the scene: *I'm up early, before anyone. I'm having devotions in the kitchen. I pause to look out the window. The sky is bright blue. White, fluffy clouds float over a panoramic view of the mountains. (Sigh!) I get out my laptop computer to catch my thoughts before they vanish.* OK—I know I'm dreaming. I have no laptop. And I'm not even a morning person.

I really wanted to buy the view home even though deep inside I knew we couldn't afford it. Suddenly I started rationalizing. *We're going to live in it for a long time so why shouldn't we get what we want? We could have people over and they could enjoy the view with us. All the elders and staff could come over for a potluck lunch and enjoy the view with us!*

It all sounded good but the bottom line was we could barely afford the house *without* the view across the street.

When Rick and I were first married, all I wanted

when it came to a home (rented or owned) was a safe, clean and cute place. Then we thought we would get a condominium. After a while, a town home sounded good. Now it's the biggie! A detached home with an attached garage.

Did you notice a trend? At first I was content with what I had. Then, somewhere along the line, I thought that a detached home with a view would make me happy.

Kirsty's pacifier may help her to feel happy for a while, but soon she will outgrow it and want her blankie or her mommy. Later, she will want to feel popular, to have a best friend, to get good grades and to be athletic. Not that any of these things are wrong, but I would want her to throw out all those false pacifiers and realize that joy comes from the fact that she is a child of God. Who could model this any better than her own mom? I have to ask myself, *Am I the woman I want my daughter to become?* Then I ask, *Would the house with a view truly make me happy?*

> **Are you the woman you want your daughter to become?**

When Kirsty gets older, she will pick up on my attitudes. She will notice how Mommy is never happy with what she has. So I've made some changes in my life. I'm working on being content with who God has made me and what He's given me.

Most importantly, I want Kirsty to see a natural outpouring of the Holy Spirit in my life that will touch her and create a desire in her to become a woman sold out to Jesus Christ.

Helpful Hint:
Write down the big ideas that you don't think you will get around to. Seeing them on paper will hold you accountable to do them!

Did you see the pacifier?

Being the woman I want my daughter to become.

Application

Write down how you want your child(ren) to imitate you.

day 2

Bubble Baths

And over all these virtues put on love, which binds them all together in perfect unity. (Colossians 3:14)

My favorite form of relaxation comes in a tub of hot water with lots of bubbles. It works!

While I was pregnant I would get into a luke-warm tub and disappear from the world. Then came baby Kirsty. After delivery I had to wait six weeks for my bubble bath. Oh, how I missed it! I would actually go into the bathroom and look at the tub and feel tempted. I did cheat a little and take my first bubble

I don't mind being in hot water—as long as it's filled with bubbles.

bath at five-and-a-half weeks. It was wonderful! Rick watched Kirsty for me. I went into the bathroom, shut the door, turned on the light and fan and started the hot water. It was a welcome break. Between the fan and the running water, I couldn't hear if the baby was crying or not.

Helpful Hint:
Here are a few items from my "creative family time" list:
1. Browse through a bookstore together.
2. Hang out on a bed Saturday morning.
3. Go for a scenic drive together.

Kirsty is now old enough to join Mom in the tub. Rick gives me ten minutes to get the water going and relax in solitude. Then he brings Kirsty in and we bathe together. She loves it! We have lots of fun splashing and playing in the water. She has her little ducky and her favorite toy is an empty bottle. I nurse her in the tub and she relaxes in my arms. This is such a precious time to bond with her.

Even more precious is when Daddy comes into the bathroom and sits on the floor next to the tub and talks with us. This is such a special time for our family. It really meets a need for Rick and me, which is to communicate without worrying about her crawling off into the kitchen or falling down. We are all content.

Did you see the pacifier?

Creative family time.

Application

List some ways your family can have creative time together. Apply these ideas at least once a week.

day 3

Maintenance

For God did not give us a spirit of timidity, but a spirit of power, of love and of self-discipline. (2 Timothy 1:7)

I remember when my doctor visits became bi-weekly. They would always check my weight first. I would step on the scale—and I had gained another pound. Finally, I got smart and stood on the scale backward so as not to see the big number. When I was admitted into the hospital, the first thing the nurse did was weigh me. I had Rick look—I couldn't. Later, I found out that I had tipped the scale to a whopping 150 pounds! I'm only 5 feet 4 inches tall! Ugh! I can still remember thinking, *I'll lose it.* I had complete confidence that I would lose the extra weight.

Soon after the baby was born I was ready to exercise. Before I became pregnant I enjoyed "jogging" (but if you were to see me out on the streets you would think I was a lady with a bouncy walk).

Helpful Hint:
Ask God to show you areas in your life you could work on. The simple things He can bring to your attention are amazing.

So I jogged afterward too. Kirsty seemed to like her baby jogger (one of those strollers with the big wheels). She was asleep by the time I was around the block. I continued to jog and go to the gym and in a few months I was back to 110 pounds. It felt so good to fit back into my jeans. I felt pretty good, too. I had a goal and I accomplished it. My baby jogger was a big help. Kind of a big, mom-sized pacifier.

But my struggle has always been maintenance. I would lose the weight and then—how about a hot fudge sundae? Or I'd clean the house all day Saturday—spotless!—and by Tuesday it's a disaster.

It's always easy to start something. It's maintaining it that's the struggle.

Did you see the pacifier?

Maintaining discipline.

Application

List problem areas in your life where you struggle with maintenence. Ask God to help you with these areas and do one activity toward maintaining discipline.

day 4

Just the Fun, Ma'am

"For I know the plans I have for you," declares the LORD, "plans to prosper you and not to harm you, plans to give you hope and a future." (Jeremiah 29:11)

"Rick, tell me about our house."

"It's a two-story and it's bigger than this place" (meaning our one-bedroom apartment).

"No, don't just give me the facts. I want to have fun and dream about it. You know, the neighborhood and all the friends we will make and how we'll have barbeques. How Kirsty will learn to ride her bike on our street. How I'll make dinner and you can be in another part of the house and I'll actually have to come looking for you. Doesn't that sound wonderful, Rick? Rick?"

Where did he go? Rick has disappeared. That figures, he's not in the mood to talk. He must have used up all his words today. I still have lots of words left. Here he is. He brought me the floor plan to our hopefully, soon-to-be home.

Don't men and women communicate differently? I wanted to just talk about our house and envision what it would be like. It's simply enough for Rick to know it's there. We do have times when we dream together about our future. We take a weekend away each year to pray and seek God's goals—His will—for our lives. It's fun to talk about them and encourage each other to take the necessary steps toward those goals. Without our dreams and goals, what would we be doing? I would probably be eating a toaster pastry, sitting on the couch watching TV. Instead, I exercised this morning and did a little writing.

> Our dreams and goals are like windows: They let light shine into our lives.

My dreams bring joy and satisfaction. There is something wonderful about beating the odds, like furthering your education or buying your first home. You see, my nature would rather have me

be a couch potato. I have to discipline myself to
take steps each day to accom-
plish the goals I've set. I have a
whole page full of goals and
dreams for the future. Will they
come true? It's up to me and
the Lord's will. You see, the fact
is it's not always fun to take the
steps to reach our goals. But
I've always found it is worth my
time.

Helpful Hint:
Realize you can
change your
goals. You
wrote them
on paper,
not in stone!

Did you see the pacifier?

*Taking time out to pray for God's will (goals) in
your family's life.*

Application

Write out your goals and post them so you can
see them daily.

day 5

The Gift of an Encourager

As iron sharpens iron,
  so one man sharpens another. (Proverbs 27:17)

Moms are the best! A close second to moms are grandmas. I think Kirsty has the most wonderful grandma in the world. Of course, I *could* be biased. My mom (Grandma Patti) came over the first week after I came home from the hospital. She helped with cleaning, cooking and, of course, the baby. We planned that when she came over I would get some sleep. Instead, it was fun to get Kirsty to sleep, sit on the couch, have iced tea and Wheat Thins and talk. Mom and I could talk from sunrise to sunset, but we both have husbands and so have to pace ourselves.

I think the hardest thing about being a mom these days is not having many working-mom role models. You see, I work full time. It really has been a struggle to figure out how to get everything done. But I have my priorities. They are: God, family, work, grocery shopping, cooking and cleaning, etc. Did you notice cleaning came in last? I do the quick pick-up and Rick cleans and does many other domestic chores. What a wonderful husband! We really do have a team approach to life.

Grandmothers are mothers who, over the years, have earned the "grand" in grandmother.

I've tried to think of someone I knew growing up whose mom worked. I just can't. Things have changed these days! What's really difficult is the books about families and motherhood discussing the positives of stay-at-home mothering, with which I have no arguments. But I know there are many women who have to work for many reasons. Where is their encouragement? I'm thankful Mom encourages me. I'm just concerned that we may have lots of women out there who don't have a Grandma Patti to encourage them. I hope I can encourage you through this book because you are all special and God will bless your desires to be a loving, caring mom.

Did you see the pacifier?

Grandmas and other encouraging women.

Application

Ask God to bring an encouraging relationship into your life.

day 6

Hot Lips

*Your beauty should not come from outward adorn-
ment, such as braided hair and the wearing of gold
jewelry and fine clothes. Instead, it should be that
of your inner self, the unfading beauty of a gentle
and quiet spirit which is of great worth in God's
sight. (1 Peter 3:3-4)*

I am thirty-three years young and I have a baby. It's
time to get myself a makeover! I've gotten a different hairstyle. I was not as daring as I intended to
be and went for the bob. (And I miss my ponytail!)
After the haircut I head for the mall. There's one
more thing I need to do now that I'm in my thirties
and a mom: Get lipstick. I notice most women wear
lipstick, and I have been wearing the same pink lip
gloss since high school. (I'm a little embarrassed to tell

you that, but I believe in honesty and transparency. I've already told you my height, weight and age. I have no idea of my measurements, but the lower you get the bigger they get.)

I went into the department store, and there were all these ladies with white coats on just waiting for me (not to take me to the hospital, rather to take my credit card). Inconspicuously, I pulled out my pink lip gloss to show the salesperson. I told her I like soft pink, but that I needed something updated. She quickly agreed. I tried on so much lipstick my lips were raw from wiping it off with the tissues. Finally, we discovered what I needed was lip liner. I put the liner on and then a darker shade of pink. I love it! I actually have lips! (You see, I have very thin lips. I always wonder when I see someone with big, beautiful lips if they're really all hers.)

How much for the lipstick? Fifteen dollars. I thought it would be around $10, but $15?! OK. How much for the lip liner? Twenty-two dollars? Wow! Forty dollars for my lips! I don't think so. I still like my frosted pink lip gloss. I figure they're still making it, so someone besides me must be buying it. So what if it's sixteen-year-old girls!

Did you see the pacifier?

Knowing your beauty comes from being God's child, not from make-up!

Application

Do you need a spiritual makeover? Ask God to give you the beauty of a gentle and quiet spirit.

day 7

A Contact Sport

*Her husband has full confidence in her
and lacks nothing of value. (Proverbs 31:11)*

"Rick, come listen to this."

"OK. I'm listening."

"Rick, put down the paper."

"OK. I'm done."

"Rick, come look at me. I want to see you."

"I'm here. We're in the same room."

"I want eye contact. I don't want you to just hear me. I want you to listen to me."

We women need a little eye contact from time to time. It's more than just the eyes; it goes

31

deeper into the soul. We want to express our-selves. We need to know someone hears and un-derstands us.

I have my ups and downs and I know Rick tries to understand me when I'm down. But I can sense when he has no idea what I'm talking about. It's at that point that I will tell him that he doesn't have to understand my feel-ings, just respect them. Then I need to call a girl-friend!

How does your husband see you in the morning? In your robe? How does he see you in the evening? In your sweats? Dress so he likes what he sees at home!

I remember when Rick and I were first married— I thought he'd come home from work and sprinkle happiness glitter all over me. He would completely understand me and meet all of my needs. That lasted, oh, a few months. Then a wonderful thing happened: I had a reality check. No man can meet all of your needs. It was very enlightening for me to realize this—and it was releasing for Rick.

As wives, we need to try to understand our men, just as we want them to understand us. Give

them a little eye contact. (Mine seems to like a little body contact too.) When we don't understand them, we must respect them. I look at it this way: Rick needs to be admired, respected and appreciated for who he is as a person, just as I do. If we don't let those wonderful men know how much we admire them, someone else will. Tonight, look that man in the eyes and tell him how wonderful he is to you.

Did you see the pacifier?

For women—eye contact, touching the soul. For men—body contact, touching him physically.

Application

Write your man a love letter—and follow it up with a hug.

day 8

Quality Time

Am I now trying to win the approval of men, or of God? Or am I trying to please men? If I were still trying to please men, I would not be a servant of Christ. (Galatians 1:10)

I love to go grocery shopping. It is the only time Rick gives me the checkbook and says, "Go shopping." He doesn't even get mad if I spend too much because I say, "Look! I bought you bagels and bananas." I've also discovered that I can write the check for $10 over the amount and get a little cash. (OK—so sometimes I write it for $20 over.) I've always enjoyed grocery shopping. Kirsty seems to enjoy it too. I lay her in the baby seat and she just watches all the canned products go by. I like to talk to her as we go. I'll tell her what the different items are as we pass them.

I remember one gloomy, cold Monday that I had the day off from work. I decided to go shopping. I had on my old grubbies, no make-up and a hat. I love those kind of days. I was doing my usual explanations to Kirsty. "This is pasta. This is fruit, and these are nuts." Everyone that walked by probably thought *I* was nuts. I didn't care; this was a special time to be with Kirsty.

Maybe all those looks in the grocery store weren't about the nutty lady. Maybe they were just admiring some good ol' quality time between a mother and her child.

Did you see the pacifier?

Just being with Kirsty.

Application

Take special time with your child, just the two of you. And do it with each child.

day 9

The Martha Complex

For you created my inmost being;
*   you knit me together in my mother's womb.*
I praise you because I am fearfully and wonderfully
*   made;*
*   your works are wonderful,*
*   I know that full well.*
*   (Psalm 139:13-14)*

One fun thing Rick and I love to do is go to
the bookstore and just browse through
various books and magazines. This must be a
popular outing because this bookstore—which is
as big as a gymnasium—has benches throughout
the store and is often crowded. Once you find
an empty bench, you really have to claim your
territory.

One of my favorite magazines to look through is *Martha Stewart Living.* I love to dream of doing some of the things she does. So far, that's all they've been: dreams. Really, who has time to do all that cooking and gardening? As I'm writing this, I have a baby crawling all over me (making adorable cooing sounds, of course).

I did have two small palm trees on our balcony. They looked great until the Santa Ana winds came, blew them over and broke the pots in which they were planted. I even had pansies planted around the bases of the trees. Have I replanted them? No.

> **The most valuable paintings are the originals. You are an original! There is no one else out there like you.**

When I think about it, it's confusing. You're wondering what the "it" is to which I'm referring. "It" refers to life and the role models we have. Martha is an OK role model but I don't need to stress out if I'm not the gourmet cook she is. I think that I have three spices in my cupboard (if you count salt and pepper). Too often, we get caught up in trying to be like someone else. If I spent my time trying to be like Martha, I would miss out on what God has for Colleen.

I don't know Martha, but I think it's safe to assume that she isn't excited about working with kids and families all week. I love being given the opportunity to minister to children and their parents. Nothing is more exciting to me than caring for people. If I used all my energy creating Martha masterpieces, I would be pretty miserable.

Helpful Hint:
Realize there are things you cannot change about yourself. Accept those things— and change the things you can!

I think one of the biggest tasks we have is to be content with who we are. If you're tall, you would rather be shorter. If you have dark hair, you imagine it would be nicer to have blond hair. If your skin is peaches and cream, wouldn't it be nice to have tan, olive skin?

The list goes on and on. It sure feels good when we get to a point in our lives when we can say, "God created me just the way I am and I like it." I can accept that I'm not crafty, logical, athletic or tall. But I am witty, creative and enthusiastic.

Did you see the pacifier?

Accepting yourself!

Application

List the qualities you like about yourself. Thank God for making you just the way you are.

Tupperware® Conscious

"The greatest among you will be your servant. For whoever exalts himself will be humbled, and whoever humbles himself will be exalted." (Matthew 23:11-12)

I 'm having a friend over for brunch. I've been cleaning the house this morning. Rick sure enjoys it when I have guests over because the house becomes immaculately clean. I take argument with that: I clean it quarterly.

My friend who's coming over is a woman in my life with whom I have had a mentoring relationship. Her children are grown and she has been married to a godly man for many years. I have valued so many of her insights.

As I've been preparing our meal, I am continually aware of how much Tupperware® I'm using (none of it matching). My friend has little crystal bowls she puts lemon slices in, and the dressing is served in another little bowl with a silver spoon. My dressing comes right out of the bottle. And my glasses have spots on them!

Helpful Hint:
Not everyone has the gift of hospitality, though many do enjoy celebrating and glorifying God in their homes. Guess what? It's OK to be casual. Don't compare your style of entertaining to anyone else's.

Reality check: Am I having my friend over to try to impress her or am I looking forward to a time of fellowship shared over a meal? (Maybe this is my Martha complex coming through.) I know the answer. I just have to keep on track.

The apartments we live in are now being sold as condominiums. They have decorated models for prospective buyers to view. So if anyone comes over to our place and I feel it is not clean enough, I tell them, "Model homes are down the street. There's no hot food or friends over there, but they are always spotless and clean."

I've loved to tour model homes for a long time; it's one of my favorite pastimes. And I finally real-

ized models are beautiful and clean because no one lives there. Amazing revelation, isn't it? Aren't closets beautiful before they get filled with our clothes, shoes, purses and belts?

Back on track. I think I need to be more interested in serving others and building friendships than in how people see me.

Did you see the pacifier?

Understanding and believing that God calls us to serve others, not impress others.

Application

Invite a friend over for tea or brunch. Enjoy serving her.

day 11

Fit for a King?

Do you not know that your body is a temple of the Holy Spirit, who is in you, whom you have received from God? You are not your own; you were bought at a price. Therefore honor God with your body. (1 Corinthians 6:19-20)

I t's been one of those days. Long, tiring, frustrating at times, and now, to top it off, I'm really hungry. I stop at the store on the way home to get disposable diapers. Guess what I see at the check-out stand? Snickers bars. Not just your regular Snickers bars but KING SIZE! I gave in, bought one and ate it on my way home. When I got home I told Rick what happened. Knowing I am trying to eat healthily and keep my weight off, he said, "You need to work on your internal discipline."

45

I replied, "Yes, but you don't know how many I *wanted* to eat."

I ate that scrumptious candy bar to relax after a hard day. I thought it would somehow make me feel better. Did it? No. I just felt guilty. But I've come a long way. You see, I used to eat one candy bar and then I would eat something else until it would snowball into a whole day of overeating junk-food. If it was Friday, I would overeat for the entire weekend. If it was near the end of the month I would eat and justify it by saying, "I'll start my diet on the first of the month." This cycle would cause me to gain more weight. I would lose the weight and start over again.

> Sometimes I'll open the fridge and just gaze. That's OK as long as gazing doesn't become grazing!

The fact is that overeating might give me a temporary relief, but in the long run it never makes me feel better. The question to ask is, *What do I really need right now?* I find the answer is not related to being physically hungry. Rather, I need to take time to do something which brings peace to my life. This could be a walk (sometimes with your little one—we're not always going to have time alone!), time in prayer, listening to music or reading a psalm or two.

Did you see the pacifier?

Realizing that our God dwells within our earthly bodies.

Application

Next time you're tired, lonely or frustrated, take time to meet your needs with God's Word.

day 12

Crockpots and Microwaves

Take me away with you—let us hurry!
Let the king bring me into his chambers.
(Song of Songs 1:4)

I love my crockpot! I can be gone all day and come home to the house smelling good, along with a ready-to-eat, hot meal. On the other hand, I love my microwave too. I can come home and in ten minutes have an entire leftover dinner heated up. These are the working woman's best friends . . . along with the dishwasher.

Women are a lot like crockpots. It takes us all day to warm up to our men. Men are a lot like microwaves. Zip and zap and they are hot. This really describes our sexual nature, doesn't it? I would like to have Rick warm me up a bit in the morning before he goes to work. Maybe a quick phone call during the day. By the time I get home, I'm warm and smelling good. I put the romantic sheets on the bed (which happen to be the *clean* sheets at our house). Rick doesn't need to be warmed up all day long like I do.

Men and women are different. The trick is learning to appreciate our differences. Women respond to touch and praise. Men respond visually. (I can look through a magazine and see all those bras, underwear and lingerie and it just doesn't do a thing for me!) As wives, we need to take care of our husband's basic needs. If we don't, someone else will. Scary, yes, but true indeed. Sometimes it's easy to think, "Now just isn't a good time." Don't wait. Go for it! (Rick is going to want to party when he reads this story.)

Helpful Hint:
Just do it!
(Rick loved
this one.)

Make sex a celebration in your marriage. God intended for husbands and wives to love one another, to be partners, to take care of each other's needs.

How can we celebrate? Here are a few ideas to stimulate your love life:

- Throw away the pajamas with feet in them.

- Shave your legs and put on a lotion that has a pleasant smell.

- Plan a date night.

- Give your bed a romantic look. (In our house, that means putting on clean sheets!)

- Get a babysitter. (Overnight would be good.)

- Tell your husband you love him and there's no one else with whom you would want to spend your life.

- Fix his favorite dinner in your honeymoon outfit. (Don't forget to shut those curtains.)

- Light the candles and turn on the soft music.

- Most importantly, pray that God would bless your relationship.

Remember, God is not a grinch when it comes to sex. He created it. I want to spend a lifetime with Rick celebrating our relationship as man and wife.

Did you see the pacifier?

Making love last and making love.

Application

Go to bed early!

day 13

Stress-buster

*"But seek first his kingdom and his righteousness,
and all these things will be given to you as well."
(Matthew 6:33)*

"**N**o" is a wonderful two-letter word. I have recently learned how to "just say no!" What a fantastic experience! Being a "yes" person all my life kept me busy with tasks in which I often wasn't very interested. I was becoming quite stressed.

Something happened when I became a mom—besides cutting my hair, filling out and getting stretch marks. I learned to say "no." Of course I always politely decline by saying, "Sounds like fun, but right now I have a full schedule."

There's an expression I really believe is true. If Satan can't keep you bad, he'll keep you busy. Often I would get so busy "for Jesus" in Bible studies, small groups, volunteer work, that I would lose my joy. I'd learned this little "method to joy" as a child:

J - Jesus

O - Others

Y - Yourself

I would get stuck on the "O" in joy and, as a result, I was exhausted trying to please all those "other" people. When Kirsty came into my life, I knew I would have to seek God's will in this area of time management. "No" became a very big part of that. I would love to be a part of the women's ministries leadership at church. I would love to be training for another marathon run or take a painting class with my friends, but I can't.

There are wonderful rewards for saying no: peace of mind; time spent with family and time to relax.

I believe life comes with seasons. I'm in the springtime. I want to watch my little flower grow. I want to water and cultivate her soil. Another season will bring a harvest. I want to be proud of the seeds I plant.

Did you see the pacifier?

Just saying no.

Application

Next time you feel pressured to do something, say, "No thanks!"

day 14

Turn Off the Talk Shows

I have seen the burden God has laid on men.
(Ecclesiastes 3:10)

Recently I took a week off of work. Kirsty and I were both sick: Kirsty with a fever and a cold, Mom with the flu. What a week! To top it off, my mom (Grandma Patti) was just as sick as we were. No relief from that corner.

By Thursday I was going stir-crazy. I couldn't sleep or eat any more soup. So I cooked a frozen pizza and turned on the TV. I was shocked at how many talk shows are on the tube! The last time I looked, there was Oprah and Donahue. I decided to count how many were in the TV guide. My total count? Approximately sixteen.

As I flipped to different shows I noticed a trend. Each show was about someone else's problems. Here are a few examples: obesity, sexual struggles, racism, affairs and, in general, people who cannot cope or get along with others. As I watched, I couldn't help but feel thankful that at least my problems weren't nearly as bad as those of all these people, who were seemingly pouring out their hearts on national television.

> A boy was at the store with his mom, and the cashier asked him if he was going home to watch the after-school special on TV. His answer was, "No, my mom said God made the sunshine for us to go enjoy!"

I once heard someone say that a talk show is like a tabloid magazine—they're not worth watching or reading! (On occasion there is probably something worthy of our time.) They target women as their audiences. Unfortunately, we are watching. Do we have nothing better to do with our time? Why do we sit and stare at the TV? Why do we sit and listen to others' problems? We could be reading a good book or investing time in our families or God.

What would happen if we un-plugged the TV? We could get plugged into a project around the house or in the community. Or better yet, we could plug into our children. Here are some suggestions:

Helpful Hint:
Plan a movie night (rent one or watch one on TV). This will make TV watching an occasion, not a habit.

- Read to your child. (Kirsty is seven months old and she will sit and listen to me as I read to her, not for long, but often.)

- Pray.

- Create a special family dinner.

- Plan a date with your husband.

- Volunteer your time to charity.

- Bake.

- Garden.

- Go to the library.

- Go for a walk.

- Go to the park.

- Make crafts with your family—color, paint, cut, glitter.

- Play a game.

- Listen to some good music.

Did you see the pacifier?

Thanking God for your life! He will not give you more than you can bear.

Application

Make your own list of family activities you can do instead of watching TV.

day 15

A Good Cry

I meditate on your precepts
and consider your ways.
I delight in your decrees;
I will not neglect your word
(Psalm 119:15-16)

Kirsty is crying. Why? She's fed, has a clean diaper, is warm and Mom is here. Trying to keep babies happy is, at times, very exhausting. They just want to be held.

Do you ever have one of those days when it would be nice to just have a good cry? Why? Just because! You've had lunch; you've gone potty. But it would be nice to have your hubby there to hold you and just have a good cry.

I had one of those days on Sunday. It was a very busy morning. We had a change in the worship service schedule, so this in turn affected the children's program schedule. I was exhausted by the end of the morning. After church and after all the kids were back in the hands of their parents, we were having a lunch for the entire congregation. I had a splitting headache and the last thing I felt like doing was being with a lot of people. To top it all off, I started my period that morning for the first time after having Kirsty and I was wearing white. A good cry was sounding better all the time.

If you're running on empty, take time to fuel up: time alone, reading, praying or writing. Keep your tank full.

A couple of aspirin, a few short hours and I'm back at home. My perspective on life is much better. Kirsty is napping and Mom is about to have a bubble bath, a good cry and then a nap.

Looking back on my busy, confusing day, I see the problem a little more clearly. The week before was hectic, and I barely had time alone to renew myself. By Sunday, I was needing to fuel up my tank to go that extra mile. I was running on empty and had nothing left to give.

Just like there's a gas station on every corner, there is also my Savior at every turn waiting to pour His Word into my tank. He provides us with the bread of life so we can go the distance.

Did you see the pacifier?

Fueling up with God's Word.

Application

Take an entire morning to yourself. Grab your Bible, pen, notebook and fuel up!

Helpful Hint:
Mornings to yourself don't happen unless you plan them. Join a baby-sitting co-op!

day 16

Joyride

He blesses the home of the righteous. (Proverbs 3:33)

One of my favorite pacifiers is a drive in the car. When I need to get out and clear my mind and have some quiet time, Kirsty and I go for a drive. Kirsty is always quiet and she usually sleeps when we go for our ride. What a joy it is to go cruising with Kirsty.

It takes about fifteen minutes to get from our house to Grandma Patti's. I take the back roads. There's less traffic and fewer stop lights. Besides, I love to drive through the neighborhood. Rick often laughs at me when I drive because I take the long way home—the way that passes a street that has big Victorian homes on it. I often look down the street to peek at the houses. I probably did this dozens of times before it occurred to me to turn down the street and look at the houses. I had the time and Kirsty had gone to dreamland. Why not?

> For a house to be a home, it doesn't have to be owned, detached or model perfect. A home is a place for families:
>
> H - Honestly
> O - Opening
>   their
>   hearts
>   and lives
>   and are
>   accepted
> M - Making
>   lasting
>   memories
> E - Encouraging
>   one another.

I saw big, beautiful homes with large front yards and darling porches that wrap around the front of the house. I drove down three streets that afternoon. It was fun and I felt satisfied.

I even enjoyed coming home to our little place. It doesn't have a porch or a yard, but it is a home. Our new oval rug we got for Christmas fits just perfectly in the family room and our welcome sign with a cow is bright and cheery. I always want our home to be a place that is a family refuge. A porch or a yard doesn't make a house a home. A home is where Mom creates a loving environment, a place where memories are formed and, most importantly, a place for a family to come together and love one another.

That afternoon's drive reminded me of my home as a young girl. The pool parties and barbecues. The many meals we shared at the kitchen table. The Christmas tree in the family room. Pulling weeds on the side yard. These may just seem like activities, but each one was done together at home with our family. My favorite memory was coming home from school and Mom being there in the kitchen. We would have a snack and I would tell her about my day.

I hope and pray that the streets I drove down today are also homes with loving moms and families. It's not the decor that counts. Rather, it's what happens within the walls and the hearts of those who dwell there.

Did you see the pacifier?

It was more than a quiet drive. It was *memories that warm the heart.*

Application

As a family, thank God for your home and ask Him to use it for His glory.

day 17

Titus Woman

Then they can train the younger women to love their husbands and children, to be self-controlled and pure, to be busy at home, to be kind, and to be subject to their husbands, so that no one will malign the word of God. (Titus 2:4-5)

MOPS. What a wonderful invention! (Not the one you use on your kitchen floor.) I'm talking about Mothers of Preschoolers organization. When I was pregnant, I could hardly wait to be a part of our MOPS ministry. I had it all planned. I would take every other Thursday morning off and attend MOPS with all the other moms. But when I was pregnant I didn't realize how hard it would be to leave Kirsty in the nursery. Kirsty could come in to the women's program with me. She would stay in her infant seat and lie quietly while I listened to the speaker and participated.

But then I tried it. You know how every sound your baby makes is magnified, each little gurgle and burp? Kirsty decided she wanted to be the speaker instead of the woman at the podium. During craft time, she felt it was time to play. What's a mother to do?

Helpful Hint:
Contact a
  M(others)
  O(f)
  P(re-)
  S(choolers)
group near you:
  MOPS International, Inc.
  P.O. Box 101750
  Denver, CO 80250-1750

Fortunately, we have a wonderful Titus woman, Sheri, in our MOPS program. A Titus woman is a godly mom who has already raised her family and offers her experienced advice to younger moms. Sheri would come at just the right time and ask to hold Kirsty. Sheri has a word of encouragement for all us moms.

I have been fortunate these past three years to have had the opportunity to develop relationships with many godly, mature women. I've spent time with different friends in their homes, listening to their encouraging words and motherly advice. Probably the most helpful moments have been

when these women have shared with me their bloopers in motherhood. I find that I can laugh at myself more easily because of their transparency.

Is there a Titus woman in your life? Let me encourage you to take the initiative and go the women's ministry leadership at your church and inquire about a Titus woman. I did something similar. I went to a friend and asked if we could get together for lunch once a month. I told her I admired her as a mother and would enjoy her input in my life. She was more than happy to make time for me.

Did you see the pacifier?

Mentoring friendships.

Application

Locate a MOPS group in your area or join a local Bible study.

day 18

No Fear

"Be still, and know that I am God." (Psalm 46:10)

Do you ever lie in bed at night and think of ways to protect your children? I often have done just that. Then I wake Rick and tell him, "When you stop to get gas, you can't leave Kirsty alone in the car when you go to the window to pay for it."

Here's a good one. "When she's older and you take her to the movies, you have to go to the bathroom before you leave home because you can't let her go into the ladies' room alone at the theater."

I used to get so worked up lying in bed thinking about how to keep Kirsty safe. I'd even get up and check to make sure the doors and windows were locked. Fear can suck the peace right out of my pacifier!

This mommy needs peace. The only way to have the peace of mind I need is to pray, to give it to the Lord. I have to give all my fears to God. My prayer for Kirsty is that she comes to know Jesus in a personal way. That she has a relationship with Jesus. That would bring her peace. I want Kirsty to carry Christ within her each moment of every day; to be empowered by the living God of the universe; to be confident because she is a child of the King; and to experience a prayer life that would give her the joy and assurance she needs to face whatever comes in life.

Wow! How exciting. I cannot think of a better way to teach Kirsty about these things than to model it myself. It brings me great peace to know that the Holy Spirit will be alive within my child. More than anything, I want to give her the power to live a full life in His love. We have such an awesome God. Instead of letting fear grip me and consume my mind, I let His presence consume me. I do this through prayer, writing, reading His Word and listening to praise music. It is true that His love casts our fear. Thank You and praise You, Jesus!

Did you see the pacifier?

Prayer, reading the Bible and spending time with Jesus.

Application

Buy a blank book (a notepad will do) and journal your prayers to God!

day 19

Ironman

"Have I not commanded you? Be strong and courageous. Do not be terrified; do not be discouraged, for the LORD your God will be with you wherever you go." (Joshua 1:9)

Each October there is a race in Hawaii called the Ironman. This is a race involving a 2.4-mile swim, a 112-mile bicycle ride and a 26.2-mile marathon run. My Ironman husband loves to do this sort of thing. We all have our own unique pacifiers. I love going to Hawaii to watch him race. This is a minimum eight-hour race, so I usually do a little shopping during the race. Some people have asked me if it's difficult being married to an Ironman. My response is, "Yeah, it's been tough going to Hawaii and it's been hard getting used to his ivory-carved abs, legs of steel and his big hairy chest."

Then there's me. Stretch marks on my legs (which resemble a road map), a tummy that is as soft as a pillow and, worst of all, the cottage cheese on the back of my thighs. It's OK. I just wear clothes that cover it all. I've never been big on wearing bathing suits. (So what's this softy doing being married to a hard-bodied Ironman?)

When Rick asked me if I would like to do a short triathlon, I thought, *No way am I going to parade this body in public!* Then something came over me, probably insanity, and I said yes. My race wasn't the Ironman. It was called the Tin Man. I carefully chose my race—one that wasn't too close to home. I had to go where I knew that no one I knew would be there. I did finish the three-mile run, ten-mile bike ride and seventy-five-yard swim.

I had two goals: The first one was to finish the race and the second was not to place last. I thought I was doing pretty well during the run; I knew I would finish. What was bothering me was the strange noise from behind. I assumed I wasn't in last place because I could hear people behind me. But when I turned around, I saw two teenage boys hanging out of the back of a truck picking up the orange cones. Oh! I was last!!

Then by the time I finished the swim, I was so

tired I couldn't even pull myself out of the pool. Rick and the lifeguard were there encouraging me. I had to go back to the other end of the pool where the steps were. I told people I just was doing a cool-down lap. That was the only triathlon I have done and I really don't have a strong desire to do another. (I don't even have a weak desire.) I do have a feeling of satisfaction knowing that I did finish one.

Sometimes people think because I'm married to an Ironman, I should be an Ironwoman. I used to feel self-conscious about this, but now I just figure the only way someone could call me an Ironwoman is while I'm getting wrinkles out of our laundry. But I keep pressing on.

Did you see the pacifier?

Realizing the Lord is with you in all you do. (I was scared to enter this race, but it was a great feeling not to let fear consume me and to go out with faith and finish!)

Application

What is it you've been wanting to try? Ask God if this might be where He's leading you.

day 20

Attitude Adjustment

"I have told you these things, so that in me you may have peace. In this world you will have trouble. But take heart! I have overcome the world." (John 16:33)

It's Sunday afternoon. Rick, Kirsty and I are enjoying a weekend away. Kirsty and Daddy are sleeping and I'm taking time to write. But I seem to be having a difficult time keeping my eyes on the paper. Stretched out before me is the Pacific Ocean. The waves are crashing on the shore and the seagulls are gliding over the sand. I'm sitting here with some hot cocoa looking out over our balcony. I see a group of boys playing soccer, couples walking hand-in-hand, a father and his daughter chasing seagulls. Outside, the palm trees are bending with the wind. All is calm and beautiful at this moment, but one can see the storm is coming closer. The clouds are hanging low over the sea, and the waves are getting bigger as they hit along the shoreline.

The calm before the storm. But I wonder if some families have the storm *before* the calm. For instance, preparing for a getaway. Let me take you back to Saturday morning. We are in the process of packing the car. Rick is getting the big items: the stroller, baby jogger, portable playpen, bouncer and the baby backpack.

OK. We're ready to go; just a few stops: the ATM, the gas station and a quick bite to eat at a taco place. Well, the ATM is out of deposit envelopes. No problem. There's another ATM a little further south. Just one question . . . where? We drive around trying to find this ATM. We stop to look in the phone book for an address, but first we have to find a telephone booth. If Kirsty were older, she would have enjoyed this scavenger hunt. But Kirsty is crying and I've got a migraine. Forty-five minutes later the check is in the bank, we have cash and we're back on the freeway.

Now that I look back, I can see that it wasn't a big deal. Why was I getting so frustrated? Why did I have a headache? I need to be a little more like the palm tree outside the window. Just bend with whatever blows my way. When there is a storm raging inside of me, I just need to relax and look forward to the calm which always seems to follow.

Did you see the pacifier?

Relaxing until the storm passes.

Application

See if your work (or husband's work) offers automatic deposit.

day 21

Dream Along . . .

He said . . . , "Listen to this dream I had. . . ."
(Genesis 37:6)

O ne of my favorite pastimes is looking at model
homes. One of Rick's favorite pastimes is looking at cars, specifically trucks. Once in a while, Rick
will ask me if I want to go look at trucks with him. My
response has usually been, "If you really want to, I'll
go." Of course he wants to, otherwise why would
he be asking? I'm ashamed to say that too many
times I have expressed my lack of interest, especially
when it comes to test-driving. But I can't even keep
track of how many times Rick has walked through
just one more model home for me just to look at the
decorations.

Many times I have said to Rick that with trying to buy a house, we can't afford to get a truck yet . . . even though I knew he was just looking. Once, Rick said in a passing conversation, "Just let me dream." Now that I think about it, I have not often been excited about what excites Rick. Maybe trucks will never excite me, but I can enjoy the time and being together. Rick has told me that I can pick out the color when we get one . . . someday. That sounds all right. A cap and carpet in the back sound nice too. Hey, I just might get excited about this truck.

I'm glad we learned to share dreams early in our marriage. I want to always dream with Rick, no matter what we're dreaming of. I once heard it said that each dream or goal is like a candle. Just light it and let it burn. I never want to blow out Rick's flame, his passion for life, his dreams.

Did you see the pacifier?

Dreaming together.

Application

Get your husband talking. Just listen and encourage him.

day 22

Seasons

Come, let us bow down in worship,
   *let us kneel before the L*ORD *our Maker.*
      (Psalm 95:6)

Being Director of Children's Ministries, Sunday often brings more than a morning of worship. I spend many mornings joining in on the worship time of our first-through-fourth-grade children. I enjoy this time of celebration and have become accustomed to the energy and joy that I experience with them.

Watching children worship brings back many memories of my childhood at church, learning to worship with my family. When I say learning, I don't mean someone told me verbally how to sit and worship. Rather, this was a time of watching and participating by imitating my parents and the other adults who also sat among us.

As a little girl I can remember sitting next to my dad at the end of the pew. I could see better sitting on the end because I could lean out into the center aisle. I can still see my dad's hands folded in his lap. I always thought they were so strong and big. I remember he would let me find the correct page in the hymn- book, even though the song would be halfway finished by the time I found it. Dad would let me put the offering envelope in the tray. Do you let your kids participate? So what if they take five seconds longer?

Helpful Hint:
In my experience, children are ready to sit through a service somewhere between ages four and seven.

When I worship today, I believe that a large part of my praises to God, by way of singing, listening and giving, are a direct result of the training I had as a child.

The family I grew up in is not currently able to worship together. As a result, Rick and I are very aware that this time in our lives, as a family unit of living and worshiping together, is a brief season. We are in the spring of our lives. Our par-

ents are in the fall of their lives. I enjoy planting the seeds of God's Word into our family. But soon enough, we will reap a harvest just as our parents did. I thank God for what He did at Calvary. Because of His great sacrifices, we can look forward to the fall of our lives, and we have the hope of eternally worshiping together as one big family.

Did you see the pacifier?

Worshiping together.

Application

Talk to your children about worship and why it is important. Plan to worship together as a family at least once a month, letting your children participate with you.

day 23

Diaper Bag Readiness

But in your hearts set apart Christ as Lord. Always be prepared to give an answer to everyone who asks you to give the reason for the hope that you have. But do this with gentleness and respect. (1 Peter 3:15)

I carry a huge pink diaper bag around. I could carry a bag half the size that I have, but I'm just one of those people who likes to go out prepared for anything. Here are a few of the things I carry in this big pink bag:

- Diapers—at least six (you never know).

- Baby wipes—a small container.

- Lotion—in case a rash appears.

- Formula—never know when hunger will strike.

- Bottles—two, just in case one breaks.

- Cheerios®—in a baggie (used for entertaining).

- Sweater—for those air-conditioned stores.

- Socks—I don't know why (maybe if the air-conditioning is on *really* high).

- Shoes—in case she wants to wear them.

- Bible or New Testament—when I need encouragement .

- Book—paperback for me (she *could* nap).

- Rattle—entertainment.

- Blanket—many uses (there's always the air-conditioning).

- Baby Tylenol®—for teething.

- Aspirin—for Mommy.

- Change of clothes—I'm prepared for the unplanned.

- Camera—for that Kodak® moment.

- Sunblock—in case we are outside.

- Hat—in case the sunblock doesn't work.

Now you will understand why my right shoulder sags.

What I discovered is that when we get home Kirsty loves to unload her diaper bag. And the more that's in her bag, the longer it takes and the more time I have to get something done. If you were to walk into our home when Kirsty has been extremely active, you would think the FBI had been there with a search warrant. The place is torn apart.

As you looked across our family room you would see a very happy baby and one mom, prepared for anything.

Being prepared gives me a sense of peace and calm. When we have to be on the run, in the spur of the moment, I just grab that huge pink diaper bag.

Helpful Hint:
Write Bible verses on index cards and put them in your car, purse, closet, kitchen —even around the bathtub!

But I also need to prepare my heart. That's why spending time in God's Word every day is so important. I'm prepared for anything—God's Word is packed in my heart!

Did you see the pacifier?

Being prepared for anything, spiritual or physical.

Application

Clean out that diaper bag and your purse. Leave only the things you *really* need.

day 24

On the Shores of the Living Water

Jesus answered him, "I tell you the truth, today you will be with me in paradise." (Luke 23:43)

For the first time, Rick and I are on our own. Kirsty is at Grandma's house for the night. Twenty-four hours of just us. This means not having to get her in and out of her car seat. No stroller, no diapers, no bottles—just us. Wow! I better be honest though. I made it about seven hours before I called to check on how she was doing. She was just fine. So with that, we were off for a long walk along the coast.

There's nothing quite like the fresh breeze of the ocean air, sand between your toes, the sunshine on your back and seagulls overhead. After our walk, we watched the sun set deep into the sky, which turned a brilliant orange. We were watching the dawn of a new day in a distant land across the world. As we sat on our lounge chairs, we people-watched. Couples walking hand-in-hand along the shore, joggers passing by, families with their dogs and—my favorite—a young family with their video camera.

Mom had the baby while Dad videotaped his daughter running and jumping in the ankle-deep water. Rick and I were trying to guess the ages of their children, whether they were from out of state or if they were just now introducing their little ones to the ocean. Then the little girl took a fall and got soaking wet, clothes and all. Mom quickly went to the stroller and seemed frustrated as she looked through her bag. She looked at her husband, who was trying to console his daughter, and told him that there were no towels. Rick walked over and handed them one of our towels and talked with the family for a bit. I was eager to see where the family was from and if I had guessed the ages of the children correctly.

As Rick sat back down next to me, he sighed. I said, "Well, are they from Kansas?"

"No, they're from nearby." He went on to explain that they had just taken their three-year-old

daughter out of the children's hospital for the day to bring her to the beach. This little girl was dying of leukemia.

Just a moment ago I was sharing in their joy, watching this young family making memories to last a lifetime. Now I share in their sorrow. This day will be imprinted in their memories forever.

My only peace and hope for them and for us (it could happen to any of us), is that heaven is filled with golden sand and shores of Living Water with the Son always embracing us. Instead of seagulls overhead, we'll hear the angels rejoice and yes, we too will join them for eternity.

Did you see the pacifier?

A place called heaven when the new day dawns. It is forever.

Application

Pray for those who may not know our Lord and Savior.

day 25

Baseball, Teepees and Telescopes

Fathers, do not exasperate your children; instead, bring them up in the training and instruction of the Lord. (Ephesians 6:4)

D ad taught me how to hit a baseball and to field a grounder. I can still hear Dad say, "Get in front of the ball, mitt on the ground. There ya go!"

Dad taught me to ride a motorcycle, to sleep in a teepee, to look through a telescope at the stars, to sweep the pool and paint the trim on the house. We only painted the trim once. The next time we hired painters.

Dad taught me to drive. I learned to be on the defensive, "Watch the other guys. Be alert." When I had my first accident, which was my fault, Dad taught me how to deal with stress. He taught me to respond to life, not to react.

Dad gave me an education . . . not just financially. He believed in me. I came home from my first year at college on academic probation. I can still remember telling the news to Dad. His response was, "You must have had a lot of fun this first year. I'm sure you'll do better next year." I ended up graduating on the dean's list.

Children's first impressions of our heavenly Father often come from their dads.

My dad gave me confidence, character, morals, values and integrity. He taught me how to grieve the loss of my oldest brother. Dad gave me strength and taught me it's OK to be afraid, although he showed me that I could overcome my fears by facing them. Today, my dad teaches me how to continue trying. Today, my dad listens as I call him and read my latest story for this book. Today, my dad is my greatest cheerleader, coach and above all, my friend.

Did you see the pacifier?

Dad.

Application

Call or write your dad today.

day 26

Dress-down Luncheon

I am not saying this because I am in need, for I have learned to be content whatever the circumstances. (Philippians 4:11)

I went to a formal luncheon the other day. I don't usually go to formal luncheons, so I didn't know what to wear. I'm the type of person who would rather blend in than stand out, so I dressed down.

There was good food, good company and good music. The catch was that I dressed way down. I had on a comfortable dress and flats while all the men were in suits and the women were power dressing. I hoped my dress didn't have any of Kirsty's drool on the shoulders. I sat through the music and then the speaker, silently punishing myself for not wearing my green suit.

> At sixteen, we worry what others think of us. At twenty-one, we don't care what they think of us. At thirty-one, we realize they weren't thinking of us in the first place!

After the luncheon, I started walking toward the back door, hoping to sneak out unnoticed. Then I heard someone say my name. She was using my maiden name. Who would be using my maiden name here? As I turned, I saw an old friend. She said, "You haven't changed a bit." I guess that's good. I told her she looked wonderful. She really did! Her response was, "I wish I could be my-self and dress like you. You never did worry about what others thought." I just smiled.

Did you see the pacifier?

Accepting yourself for who you are and learning to be content in all circumstances.

Application

Ask yourself these questions:

1. What do I need (not want) to be content?

2. What steps do I need to take in order to make #1 happen?

Helpful Hint:
Take time each day to ask God to give you peace and contentment. Go to His Word often for encouragement. He will give you joy in the day-to-day routine!

day 27

Little Princess

Whatever you do, work at it with all your heart, as working for the Lord, not for men, since you know that you will receive an inheritance from the Lord as a reward. It is the Lord Christ you are serving. (Colossians 3:23-24)

At times I look at Kirsty and I'm overwhelmed with joy. I still can't believe this little girl is my precious daughter and that I have the privilege to raise her and be her mother.

I look forward to her first understandable words, her first kiss on my cheek, her first hug, the first picture she will color for Mommy, her first pair of frilly underwear—and the list goes on.

Even though I look forward to all these special moments, I am in love with this present moment. It seems as though just yesterday I was looking forward to her first steps, first tooth, first bottle, first babbling, first solid food, first bathing suit, first giggle, first opinion, first wave, first barrette in her hair.

I am already looking back, enjoying my memories of Kirsty. In two weeks she will be one year old. Unbelievable, but true. Time does fly by when you're having fun.

My goal each day is to just enjoy the present moment and pour all my love and wisdom into this little WOG (woman of God). I so much want her to grow up knowing that she is special, that she is loved and that she is a daughter of the Most High, the King of kings, our Lord Jesus Christ.

Yes, Kirsty is a little princess. I will show her how to live as a daughter of the King and give her a heritage that comes from God's Word. She too will join in His riches and everlasting treasure. I will teach her that she can inherit the kingdom of heaven by simply becoming His daughter.

Did you see the pacifier?

You are a royal princess with a wonderful inheritance.

Application

Take a moment to bow to your King and give Him thanks.

day 28

Party!

*This is the day the LORD has made;
let us rejoice and be glad in it. (Psalm 118:24)*

Let's party! I love those two words. They mean "let's have a good time." I believe God intended for His children to know how to party.

When I was teaching preschool, each day we had scheduled potty breaks and when I would say, "Let's go potty," Ginny would jump up and down and say, "Yay! A party, a party!" This little four-year-old attitude would take on energy, excitement and anticipation. I wonder why we don't have this type of attitude as adults?

Actually, I don't have to wonder. I realize we all have financial worries and health problems, and sometimes our daily struggles seem to smother us—although, every now and then I meet someone who seems to rise above the everyday trials. This person seems to truly enjoy and embrace life.

I desire to model for Kirsty a party attitude. For me this simply means rejoicing in the Lord always. Each day I want Kirsty to wake up, look up to her Lord and say, "I love You. I'll walk with You and I rejoice in You." Each day is to be lived as an adventure in her faith.

How can we teach our children to do this? By doing it ourselves. The question is *how* do we do this. I can share with you what I do. First, I don't expect life to be problem-free. I face my struggles and solve them while they are little. I tell the people I work with that I like little problems. Give me the little ones and please don't wait until they're big. Next, I look at problems as an opportunity to grow and watch God work in each situation. Last, I wake each morning with the living God of the universe and greet Him by praising Him and thanking Him for the many blessings we have. Here are a few blessings:

- Our home.

- Our healthy baby.

- My faithful husband.

- Grandparents close by.

- Cars that run.

- Food in the refrigerator.

- A church family.

Did you see the pacifier?

Rejoicing in the Lord!

Application

List all the things you are thankful for. Have the entire family create a list. Post it on the refrigerator.

day 29

SOS Plan

*Enter his gates with thanksgiving
  and his courts with praise;
  give thanks to him and praise his name.
    (Psalm 100:4)*

Rick, Kirsty and I drive to church along a quiet, secluded road. We take our time and enjoy the scenery. Kirsty enjoys her bottle while we enjoy praise music to prepare our hearts for worshiping our Lord.

I like to change gears for Sunday mornings. It seems to be my job to set the mood and the pace for the day. In order for the mood and pace to be comfortable and enjoyable, I get ready early. When I'm ready, I can then focus on getting Kirsty up, dressed and fed without a frenzy. (Rick is on his own.)

I have to add that I learn quickly. You see, the first six months after Kirsty was born, there was no peace on Sunday mornings. This was not going to become our standard. But how would I change it so it didn't continue?

The last thing I want our children to be worried

Habits are like comfortable beds: easy to get into and hard to get out of.

about on Sunday is, *Will Mom be together enough to get us together for church?* I envision my children crying and arguing about what they will wear, all of us trying to get a hot shower in the same hour and my giving them do-nuts to eat in the car on the way there, shouting at them

not to drop the crumbs all over the car seats. No way would this be the future of our day of rest. "Be solution-oriented" has become my motto!

Here is my step-by-step plan to a wonderful Sunday. Yes, even if you are on staff at a church, you can enjoy the Lord's day.

Solution on Sunday (SOS) Plan

1. Saturday evening

   a. Begin to prepare our hearts through prayer and Scripture

   b. Shower/bathe kids

    c. Choose outfits

    d. Go to bed early

2. Sunday morning

    a. Mom up before everyone else to get ready physically and spiritually

    b. Mom prepare breakfast before anyone is up—cereal, oatmeal, something easy

    c. Family eat together

    d. Dress and go

    e. Drive to church, talking about family day together

While we have young children, we plan to spend Sunday together, focused on our Lord and family. This may mean a picnic in the park, a day at the pool, coloring at the kitchen table or going to the beach. I just don't want our family days to slip by us without creating special memories. This includes our Sundays being fun and Spirit-filled.

Did you see the pacifier?

Family days.

Application

Plan your next Sunday to be with family and worship together.

day 30

First Birthday

*Fix these words of mine in your hearts and minds.
. . . Teach them to your children, talking about
them when you sit at home and when you walk
along the road, when you lie down and when you
get up. (Deuteronomy 11:18-19)*

I can't believe Kirsty is one year old! It seems like
yesterday that we were leaving the hospital.
This has been the most rewarding year of my life. I
have grown and learned so much.

The evening after Kirsty's first birthday I sat and
reflected on all the things I have learned and the
things that I want her to learn too.

Life is made up of time.

What I do each day matters. If I leave the TV on

or the beds unmade, Kirsty will imitate these habits. I also need to get the most out of nap time (hers, not mine). About ninety percent of this book was written during nap time. Kirsty's nap is two hours each day, which averages out to 600 minutes each week, 3,000 minutes each month and 36,000 minutes each year.

> Time management is nothing more than life management. Life is made up of time.

Process is important.

I catch myself thinking often about the outcome of Kirsty's life and I forget the day-to-day tasks which will bring about our goals. For example, I hope Kirsty will enjoy the outdoors. If I don't take the time to enjoy walks, then she might not learn to enjoy them either. I can get so busy reading or doing adult-oriented activities that I forget to just get down and get dirty with Kirsty.

Take time to laugh.

I love to hear Kirsty giggle uncontrollably. Her face lights up, her seven teeth are visible and her high-pitched giggle is absolutely adorable. I noticed one day she was imitating my laughter. It not only melted my heart, it also broke it. Had I not noticed her laugh before because I was too busy? I need to

teach her to laugh and enjoy life by modeling this for her.

Be disciplined.

I desire to live a disciplined life so that Kirsty will learn to be disciplined in her life also. I want Kirsty to develop the spiritual disciplines of prayer, meditating on God's Word, worship and stewardship. I desire for Kirsty to be able to say "no" to time-wasters and "yes" to the goals she sets for herself.

Set goals.

From a very young age, I want Kirsty to set goals and feel the satisfaction of doing her best. I believe this process has already begun. I will allow Kirsty to work at something and achieve it without my making it easy for her. Kirsty *worked* at climbing on the couch. She struggled at first and grunted. Her facial expression was intense! But today she climbs up with ease. If I had lifted her each time, she would not have felt the feeling of satisfaction. This afternoon she put her toy on the couch, then climbed up, sat next to me and grinned. I will help her to focus on goal-setting and she won't even know it. A few goals we'll start with will be:

- Earn a star each day on her chore chart.

- Learn to play one song on the piano.

- Improve her reading.

- Count to ten.

- Swim two laps without stopping.

Wake up each morning with Jesus.

This is number one! I want Kirsty to live moment by moment with the Lord Jesus. As her mother, I want to model a relationship with Jesus and for her to know she has the Spirit of God within her. I want Kirsty to be empowered by God to be bold and courageous. Once again, I realize someone must teach her this. I have the greatest privilege and the greatest task of all, which is to raise a child to love her God with all her heart, with all her mind and with all her soul.

Did you see the pacifier?

Parenting with purpose.

Application

Write out your goals/purposes regarding raising your children.

day 31

Directions for a Trip to the Mall

"Knock and the door will be opened to you." (Matthew 7:7)

Taking your little one to the mall is always an adventure. For more fun, follow these simple directions.

Find a place to park (after only four or five trips around the mall). Gingerly open the car door, trying not to hit that beautiful sports car (washed and freshly waxed) parked next to you. Fight and conquer the stroller as it resists coming out of the trunk. If you are unfortunate enough to have a two-door car, climb into the back seat to unlatch, unhook or unbuckle the baby from the car seat.

Can't find the car keys? Look on top of the car. No? How about on the car seat? No? Check the diaper bag where you put them. When you sense that you have an audience—the owner of the car inevitably parked on the other side of you, waiting patiently for you to finish up and move on out—look more frantically for the keys. Double-check before you shut the door to make sure you actually have them. Get the bottle. You're on your way for a few moments of relaxation.

Helpful Hint:
Girls between eight and twelve years old are too young to baby-sit, but they often like to be a helper for a day or a few hours.

Obstacle ahead: Get ready to enter The Mall Door. Nonchalantly try to time your entry with a friendly-looking person who wouldn't seem to mind holding the door open. If no such person is available, get some momentum going and swirl the stroller around while at the same time quickly opening the door with one arm, wheeling the stroller in backward. If the door is heavy, use your entire body to hold the door open and hope the width of the doorway is large enough for both the stroller and you. Of course, the preferred option—and a wonderful mom-sized pacifier in these conditions—would be the friendly passerby.

If you've never had the above experience, just stand outside of any mall and observe moms with strollers—or handicapped folks with wheel-chairs—entering. Don't forget, you could be a Good Samaritan and open the door for the shop-per in distress.

Did you see the pacifier?

Automatic doors or helpful passersby (spiritually speaking, Good Samaritans!).

Application

Watch and help those in need of door assis-tance.

day 32

Water Filter

"Whoever believes in me, as the Scripture has said, streams of living water will flow from within him." (John 7:38)

Can you believe that for the first nine months of Kirsty's life I boiled her water to get rid of the germs? Yes, this was a hassle! Then it occurred to me that I probably couldn't boil the lead out of the water. What I needed was a water filter.

It was especially annoying when Rick would come home and accidentally drink her water. I remember when we first got married and I went through explaining to him that these certain bath towels are just for looks; they are too pretty to dry your hands with. These pot holders are not to be used; they hang as decorations. And now I'm telling him he can't drink the water.

I have often wondered: What needs to be filtered out of my life? The only way I can keep my life clean is to keep my heart and mind in a constant relationship with Jesus. As clean, refreshing water pours out of our spring water bottle, I want His Spirit to pour through me to cleanse me. Only then can I truly satisfy the needs of my family. Oh, to give Kirsty a taste of the Living Water which only comes from knowing Jesus.

Did you see the pacifier?

When Jesus filters sin out of my life and cleanses me.

Application

Set aside some time for heart-searching and repentance with the Father.

day 33

Sonblock

To the Jews who had believed him, Jesus said, "If you hold to my teaching, you are really my disciples. Then you will know the truth, and the truth will set you free." (John 8:31-32)

Ultraviolet rays. Gotta keep them off my baby's precious, fair skin. So what was I doing here at Rick's triathlon, which would take him close to four-and-a-half hours to complete? There was no shade except for in the cement areas. I tried to fashion a tent covering with our little umbrella stroller. *Tried* is the key word. And Kirsty wouldn't keep a hat on. So I drenched her in sunblock, hoping this would do the trick.

The clouds did appear later in the afternoon. Relief . . . so I thought. Rick told me later that the UV rays go through the clouds. I should have known that. Kirsty's chubby little cheeks were pink, matching her little pink nose. I felt so bad. Every time she fussed or cried I assumed it was her sunburn.

In my teenage years I tried to get a suntan every summer. Now that I'm beginning to wrinkle, I don't think that sunbathing was such a good idea. Today I wear hats and lots of sunblock. Really, the damage has already been done. I have the scars to show it. My skin looks a tad bit like my leather purse. Thanks to make-up—foundation, to be exact—I'm human-looking again.

The grass may look greener on the other side, but remember: Their water bill is higher.

Speaking of foundation, can we give our children—daughters, specifically—a firm foundation so they don't have to go through those silly rituals of sunbathing or dieting to feel beautiful and special? I believe we can. While our children are young, we need to begin letting them know they are wonderfully made and we love them just as they are.

Many myths exist that really block our relationship with the Son. I call these myths Sonblock. We think we'll be loved if we are beautiful, successful, wealthy, athletic, etc. Myths—all myths. If you are

searching for the world to love you, then your journey will be long and hard, and you will never arrive. If you can join me in seeking His love, you will experience contentment and joy like no other.

Did you see the pacifier?

Using God's Word to block the myths the world is trying to feed us. If we buy into the world's lies, we will be burned by its empty philosophies.

Application

Memorize John 8:31-32. Write it on an index card and put it on your bathroom mirror.

day 34

Mother's Day

Her children arise and call her blessed;
her husband also, and he praises her:
"Many women do noble things,
but you surpass them all."
(Proverbs 31:28-29)

Recently I spoke at a women's conference, where I had shared that I desire for my children to call me blessed. A lady, whose age I would guess to be around eighty, volunteered to share an example of how her son had called her blessed.

She began by telling us that she had always taught her son about honesty, integrity and a strong work ethic. Now that her son had his own successful business, he had applied these character traits to his life and work.

One afternoon her son made a lunch appointment with his mom, and the two sat talking about his business.

"I recently had an opportunity to make an incredible deal, Mom," he told her. "It would have made me richer than any deal I had ever made if I didn't mind a little dishonest business and a few white lies."

No matter how you look at it, forward or backward, you're always "Mom."

But then the son gave his mom a bouquet of flowers he had hidden under the table. He reached for her hand, kissed her and said, "Thanks, Mom, for teaching me to be an honest man, husband and father."

After he drove her home and walked her in, he said, "I love you, Mom."

Of course we were all in tears when she finished the story. She concluded by saying, "That afternoon my son called me blessed—in his own words."

My daughter is still too young to call me blessed, but I desire to live my life so that someday she will bear the fruit of my ministry and my life invested in hers.

Did you see the pacifier?

Live the words of Proverbs 31:10-31.

Application

Call your mother! Tell her you love her!

day 35

Simple Gifts

The LORD *protects the simplehearted. (Psalm 116:6)*

So many toys, so little time. (Kirsty outgrows and out-interests them all.) And so little space to put them all.

What Kirsty really likes, better than her toys, is the boxes in which her toys come. As I am writing this, she is happily sitting in her box. Yesterday I brought a box home to pack her clothes in. No way. As soon as Kirsty recognized this new toy, she was all over it. All those expensive toys she got for Christmas—her toy phone, cash register, books, blocks and stuffed animals—didn't matter. The box was her delight.

Maybe I need to remember to keep it simple. It's not the most expensive things in life that bring us joy or happiness. What makes Kirsty happy is a clean dia-per, a bottle, being with her mommy and daddy, bubble baths and, of course, feeling safe, clean and content.

Bumper sticker: "Live simply so others may simply live."

Funny, things don't really change a whole lot as we grow older. What truly brings me joy isn't designer clothes or gourmet food, which I don't have anyway. What matters to me most are simple things: the times I play and laugh with Kirsty—and, of course, those mom-sized pacifiers like:

1. Exercise—Great for releasing a little tension.

2. Television—Wonderful for zoning out.

3. Phone—A line of communication for an adult conversation.

4. Book—Escape from laundry and dirty dishes. It works if they all nap at the same time.

5. Bubble bath—Soak it up and pamper your-self.

6. Shopping—Grab the stroller and keep it moving before your baby jumps out.

7. Ice cream—Indulge yourself then go back to #1.

8. Nap time—Not you, the kids. You get to re-lax.

9. Baby-sitter—Establish the baby-sitter before she (or he) establishes a social life.

10. When the church bulletin reads "child care provided." (Unless of course, the children's ministries director calls and asks you to vol-unteer in the nursery.)

Kirsty has taught her mommy an important lesson. She taught me that it's the simple things in life that bring true joy and con-tentment. For example, it is Sat-urday evening. Rick is reading. Kirsty is still playing in her boxes and I am here writing. I am content tonight with my family. What a joy!

Helpful Hint:
Make your own list of the simple things you enjoy doing. Then thank God for them!

Did you see the pacifier?

Enjoying the simple things in life.

Application

Keep receipts for everything. Return what your children don't like!

day 36

Sit with the Savior

The LORD is my shepherd, I shall not be in want.
He makes me lie down in green pastures,
he leads me beside quiet waters,
he restores my soul. (Psalm 23:1-3)

I came home from work today discouraged. Why?

- Not enough sleep the night before.

- Forgot to pack lunch, no money in wallet.

- Strained chicken is pretty bad.

- The material I ordered was lost in the mail.

- Have to go to a meeting tonight.

When I'm discouraged, it is usually because I am hungry and thirsty. Not physically, but spiritually. The signs of my spiritual hunger surface in loneliness, discouragement, depression, hopelessness and lack of motivation.

I have been sitting on the couch for the last thirty minutes writing, praying and reading. Wow! I actually feel peace. I don't have that heavy feeling inside my stomach. All because I took time to sit with my Savior and rest with Him in His Word and prayer. I guess that's what God means when He tells us, "My grace is sufficient for you, for my power is made perfect in weakness" (2 Corinthians 12:9).

> In the middle of "discouragement," you find "courage." That's exactly what it takes to rise above our circumstances.

Did you see the pacifier?

Sitting with the Savior each day.

Application

Stock snacks in your purse or at the office for the day you might forget your lunch!

day 37

Spiritual Make-up

Stand firm then, with the belt of truth buckled around your waist, with the breastplate of righteousness in place. (Ephesians 6:14)

I try to be as natural as possible. All of my body is mine. You know, no implants. My one and only vice, when it comes to appearance, is make-up. I need the Clinique.® When I get out of bed in the morning and look at myself in the mirror, I see this pale, dull, colorless face. Yet, after a shower, some mousse, blow drying, curling iron and make-up, I join the living. I don't even need a cup of coffee. OK, maybe a diet cola. This routine can be done in thirty minutes.

Many a morning I stop to ask myself, *Are you*

ready for this day spiritually? I just spent thirty minutes on the outward appearance. How about my heart and my attitude? One day after asking myself this question I walked back into the house and

How much time do you spend getting ready physically each morning? How much time do you spend getting ready spiritually?

picked up my Bible and said, "OK, God, I want to be beautiful on the inside too." I began to put on my foundation with God's Word. Then I added some joy and color to my countenance by praising Him. Next the mascara, by committing it to memory so my eyes could truly see the truth all day long. Lastly, the perfume of His presence, His Spirit with me all day.

I can still remember the day I walked back in to get my Bible. Boy, did I need it too. I had no idea of the events that were about to take place. If I hadn't taken the time to get spiritually ready, I think I might have really embarrassed myself by losing my temper.

We don't know the events of the days ahead of us. But we can prepare by applying a firm foundation in our lives by getting ready spiritually as well as physically.

Did you see the pacifier?

Wearing the most costly fragrance there is . . . His Spirit.

Application

Buy yourself some fragrant lotion. When you put it on, remember to ask the Holy Spirit to fill you with His beauty.

day 38

Hubby First

A wife of noble character is her husband's crown.
(Proverbs 12:4)

Sometimes I forget to think of Rick's needs. I get so caught up being a mom that being a wife takes second place. This must be difficult for our husbands since they used to be number one. I now have a list of things to do for Rick to show him he's number one. I asked myself, *What would make Rick happy? How can I show him I love, respect and admire him?* Let me share with you a portion of my "things to do for Rick" list.

- Note in his lunch.

- Cook his favorite meal.

- Get a baby-sitter for a planned date.

- Great sex . . . why not? We're married!

- Listen to him.

- Go look at trucks with him and be interested.

- Drive on our next date.

- Rent a movie he would like to see.

- Make him king for the day (do whatever he wants).

I really like to do these little things for Rick because it cheers him up. Isn't it great to be married to a happy husband?

Did you see the pacifier?

Putting hubby first.

Application

Pick two of the above and do them this week.

day 39

Taming the Tube

After this, Jesus traveled about from one town and village to another, proclaiming the good news of the kingdom of God. (Luke 8:1)

I have some good news and some bad news. First, the good news. If you don't like where you're living or you don't like your job, it will change. Now the bad news. If you love where you are in life, your home, the ages of your children, that too will change.

Speaking of news, have you noticed the news on TV lately? It's more like the gossip column. I can't tell you how many times I've listened to the news and thought, *This sounds just like a talk show.* Who determines what news or information will get reported? Could it be us? If we're watching it, they'll continue to cast it our way, hook, line and sinker. That's sometimes how we react to the media.

Instead of turning the news on to see what the royal family is doing or which celebrity did what, I choose my news by reading the newspaper. In order for our family to do this, I felt we needed to have a plan. I call our plan "taming the tube."

Here's our approach. We use a yellow highlighter and mark on the TV schedule what we desire to watch. We post it and, most importantly, we stick to it. The TV doesn't get turned on in between those times. We really don't need to go through this procedure very often because the few shows we do watch are weekly.

Wouldn't it be wonderful if there were a thirty-minute news program that only reported good news? Stories of people caring for others. Maybe if we let the ratings go down, they'll catch our vision for good news. Until then, why don't we act as the newscaster and share some good news? (How about His News?)

Did you see the pacifier?

Sharing some Good News.

Application

Ask God to place a name of someone upon your heart who needs to hear the Good News. At the right time, share with them God's love.

day 40

Oil Change

Be filled with the Spirit. (Ephesian 5:18)

oday Kirsty and I had to do my least favorite
chore. We took my car to have the oil
changed. Kirsty wanted so badly to get a close-up
look at our car, which was overhead. Kirsty is the
type of baby who doesn't want to watch anything
happen. She would rather make it happen.

I decided I would walk with her through the obstacle course of tires. We stood in the big tire-filled
garage watching all that old oil come gushing out.

It only took fifteen minutes to do the work on
my car. As I waited, I thought about the old oil
spilling out of my car and the new oil they put in. I
found myself wishing I too could just let all the bad,

old, negative oils pour out of me and then fill up with some new, fresh, ready-to-go oil. If only we could go in for an oil change to get rid of all those pollutants.

Helpful Hint: Check the oil in your car. (Or ask your husband to!)

Wait a minute. It *does* work that way after all. Christ is always there for us to refill our hurting, struggling hearts. He's our great mechanic with His tool, the Holy Spirit, ready to fill and clean our hearts. Never any waiting either.

Did you see the pacifier?

Free refills.

Application

When we need to refill our hurting hearts is when we don't feel like doing it. Fill up with His love daily so you're never on empty!

day 41

Picture-perfect?

But godliness with contentment is great gain. (1 Timothy 6:6)

Picture day! I took Friday off from work to have Kirsty's photo taken. The morning started out serenely enough. Kirsty played for a while on our bed. We had breakfast together, a bubble bath— and then the fun started.

Usually getting dressed isn't a problem. But today Kirsty didn't want her diaper changed, her tights on or her dress over her head. And no way was she going to leave her matching head-band on.

Our appointment was for 2 o'clock. Of course, we were running late. What else could go wrong?

Kirsty's nose started to run and if I tried to wipe it she would cry. She hadn't had a nap all afternoon, which is not good for her disposition. *OK. I'll calm down and give her a bottle,* I thought. Next, her bottle opened and spilled all over her. I was beginning to think that this was not going to be picture day after all.

They say a picture is worth a thousand words. If pictures could talk, I wonder how much we would learn about someone. I look at our wedding picture. It says bliss. I look at the picture of our family right after Kirsty was born. It says joy. I look at the picture of me right after the Los Angeles Marathon. It says exhausted. I look at the picture of Rick after the Ironman Triathlon. It says, "I finished!"

What do you see when you look at the pictures in your photo album? It always helps me to remember nothing is picture-perfect. Actually, nothing is perfect, though we live in a culture that promotes perfection. It's no wonder so many of us are not happy with what we look like or what we have.

Someday, when I'm an elderly woman, I would like to look back on our family album and see joy, peace and His love spilled over the pages. I would like my life to tell His story.

Did you see pacifier?

Realizing that nothing is picture-perfect.

Application

Take another picture—you can never have too many. Have a portrait of yourself and the kids done and give it to your husband for his wallet.

day 42

Laugh a Little

Rejoice in the Lord always. I will say it again: Rejoice! (Philippians 4:4)

One of my favorite things to do is to try and get Kirsty to giggle. There is nothing sweeter than an eight-month-old baby giggling. I'll kiss her tummy, play peek-a-boo, do my Yogi Bear imitation, and she's laughing. When Kirsty laughs, I smile. I'll work as hard as I have to for a good giggle from my baby.

There are people who make a living just getting us to laugh. We pay money to hear people who will, in turn, put a smile on our face. There are shows on TV that are geared toward laughter. I wonder if laughter is supposed to come easily?

When I was teaching junior high, I can remember laughing in front of my class one day. The class started to laugh also. Then I couldn't stop laughing. I was laughing so hard that I was in tears. My students were laughing just as hard. I have no idea what we were laughing about, but it must have been funny at the time. I can still remembertellingthestudents, "Let's pull ourselves together and get back to work." Only one problem, though: I couldn't keep a straight face. But I have to tell you—that was one of the most fun days of my career.

Helpful Hint:
At times we don't feel like rejoicing, let alone laughing. Try getting out your old photo albums— those horrible oldhairstyles can be pretty funny!

I ran into three of my students recently after four years had passed. Guess what they remembered about our class? What else—the day none of us could stop laughing!

Did you see the pacifier?

Laughing a little.

Application

Buy a good clean joke book. Share a joke or two with your family and friends.

day 43

User-friendly

A patient man has great understanding. (Proverbs 14:29)

A few years ago, Rick decided it was time for the Mountains to own their first computer. We started visiting computer stores to investigate which brand would be best for us. Visiting computer stores, for me, ranks right up there with shopping for trucks. I did learn something from all those trips to computer stores: Single women looking for a man should start shopping for a computer. There are guys all over the place!

Rick is the type of consumer who will research the product thoroughly, read consumer reports and everything else on the subject. Rick could have been a computer salesman by the time we were ready to buy one. We chose our system carefully. The only thing I know about the computer we purchased is that it is IBM-compatible.

I use the computer for letter-writing and other simple tasks. I work on word processing. Rick has some other graphic programs, but I haven't invested the time into learning about them. Rick keeps telling me I can learn these programs because they are user-friendly.

User what? "Friendly," Rick keeps telling me. Hmm . . . how about a friendly husband who just puts the information in the computer for his dear wife?

I've been using a yellow legal pad and a ball-point pen to write this book. Rick tells me how much easier it would be to just type it on the computer in the first place. I don't think so. I can get comfortable on our sofa, put the afghan over my lap (I'm always cold, but that's another story) and write to my heart's content.

Did you see the pacifier?

When your husband is patient with you.

Application

Do you try your husband's patience? Take some time to examine your attitudes and ac-

tions. Try asking your husband how you can improve your user-friendliness!

day 44

Joy in the Journaling

Train a child in the way he should go,
and when he is old he will not turn from it.
(Proverbs 22:6)

One of my favorite pastimes is writing. I love to spend time reflecting on my experiences and putting them down on paper. It is pure joy to have a quiet moment with pen and notepad. Recently I have discovered the other half of this joy—reading my old journal entries. My journals go back to my teenage years. This has been very embarrassing. Boy, was I full of emotions! I'll have to make sure to state in my will to burn the box in the garage labeled "journals."

This past year I have received great satisfaction keeping a journal for Kirsty. I desire to give her so much, and since my life span is unknown, I want to make sure it is on paper. I also want her to have in writing what my vision is for her.

> Goals that are not written down are only wishes. We know our wishes don't always come true. Take time to write out your goals.

I will never tell her what to be when she grows up (in the sense of her interests and goals), although I will influence her in character, morals, values, lifestyle, goal-setting, work ethic and, most importantly, a life inspired by the Almighty, powerful God. Whoever said motherhood isn't the most powerful position one could hold? We train, delegate, keep a budget, influence and our position is in great demand. Below is one of my journal entries to Kirsty.

March

Dear Kirsty,

You are sleeping in your crib. I have about thirty minutes to myself. I could either

talk on the phone, clean the bathroom or write in my journal to you.

Life is full of choices. Each choice we make is an investment into who we become. As life is filled with choices, our days are filled with time. What we do with our time each day helps us to choose who we become. Who we become has largely to do with our goals. Goals are simply those things we want to accomplish. Goals should be written down on paper. A goal that is not written down is simply a wish. We know that wishes don't always come true.

Sweetheart, I know you can reach all the goals you set for yourself. You see, goals are an expression of who we are, who God made us to become. We all have different goals and interests. That's because God made each of us unique and special.

It is my prayer that you learn to accept who you are in the family of God. May you find what you love to do and allow God to work through your life to glorify Him.

Hugs and kisses,

Mom

Helpful Hint:

Wondering how to start journaling? Just write! Do it once a week or once a month. Don't worry if it's not perfect. And if you can't think of anything to say, then open your Bible and write your child a verse. God will bless your efforts.

Did you see the pacifier?

Leaving a personal legacy for your children.

Application

Buy a blank book for each child—start writing today!

day 45

Career Mom

She considers a field and buys it;
out of her earnings she plants a vineyard.
She sets about her work vigorously;
her arms are strong for her tasks.
(Proverbs 31:16-17)

I have spent much energy trying to figure out if I should feel guilty for working outside our home. First, I must say that if I didn't have to work I probably wouldn't. But that is not my situation, so I have learned to accept it. I believe it has been difficult for me because my family resembled that of Ozzie and Harriet Nelson. Great memories, I might add. You see, my mom was the best! She was always there for us as nurse, tutor, costume designer, coach, cheerleader and advisor.

I too want more than anything to be there for my children. I'm extremely blessed to have been able to nurse Kirsty and bring her into work with me. I can only accept this as God's blessing my desire to be a mother who glorifies Him. I don't use my paychecks to buy designer clothes, a leather briefcase or to make payments on fancy jewelry. Not that these things aren't attractive to me at times.

> Who we become is largely due to how we spend our time.

When I came to accept that I am a career mom, I actively got better at motherhood. I discovered I could lead by example. You see, there is a good possibility that Kirsty will also work outside the home. I can blaze a trail for her to follow. The greatest struggle I have is trying to live up to the example my mom set. God has given me peace as I am a pioneer in making a trail for career moms.

I add this last chapter because there is so much debate between career moms and noncareer moms. I believe all moms need to come together and support each other. Here's an idea: Stay-at-home moms could adopt a working mom and working moms could help a stay-at-home mom by taking her kids to dinner—our favorite restaurant, McDonalds.® A stay-at-home mom has adopted me. She drops off homemade bread at my home and records programs with family topics for me to watch later. What a blessing she is.

I trust God is using my life, even my work, to raise up a young WOG (woman of God). As I have been clearing my own trail, I have to say that I'm getting better each day. I believe we are at a crossroads in parenting. As we enter the twenty-first century, we will do things differently from the way our parents did. Because they are different, doesn't make them right or wrong.

Did you see the pacifier?

Trailblazing!

Application

Adopt another mother and encourage her as you both walk with God.

Epilogue

Since I started writing this book, I have come a long way in this journey we call motherhood. I am learning to take life one day at a time. In fact, I'm learning to take life one night at a time. You see, my children (yes, I now have two) are nocturnal. They don't believe in sleep. Oh, how I wish I could bottle up their energy!

I should take a moment to introduce you to my son, Luke Russell Mountain. He is two years old and all boy. Luke and I were in the bath just moments ago splashing in the bubbles when Luke said, "Poo poo, Mommy!" Yes, he pooped in the tub! So there I was on my knees scooping out little brown balls. (Gross, I know!) That bath was not nearly as relaxing as I had hoped.

It is now 9:30 p.m. Both Kirsty and Luke are in bed for the night. Time for me to catch a few moments alone reading and writing . . . so I thought. I hear the pitter-patter of little feet coming down the stairs. I read them one last story from our toddler Bible and put them back to bed.

In my attempt to be alone, I retreat to my closet to read, thinking that they won't see the light beaming from under the closet door. Well, here we are, the three—no, four—of us in the walk-in closet. Rick has decided to join us too. Kirsty's enthusiasm to act out her Bible story has got the best of us. Have you ever had the Last Supper in your closet using pretzels and paper cups?

These days (and nights), quiet moments are rare and far between, but I wouldn't trade my calling in life as "Mom" for anything else.